How Do I Play Games Online?

Tricia Yearling

How Do I Play Games Online?

Tricia Yearling

Enslow Publishing
101 W. 23rd Street
Suite 240
New York, NY 10011
USA

enslow.com

Words to Know

account—A membership to a Web site.

avatar—An icon that represents you online.

download—To add files from a Web site to a computer.

gamer—Someone who plays online or video games.

griefer—A gamer who is a bully.

Internet browser—Software that lets people use their computers to see Web sites.

Internet connection—Something that connects a computer to the Internet.

moderator—Someone who makes sure that people get along.

network—A group of connected computers.

video-game console—A tool that lets people play video games.

Contents

Words to Know 4

Chapter 1: Do You Want to Play a Game? 7

Chapter 2: Different Types of Games 11

Chapter 3: Gaming Safety 18

Chapter 4: Set Limits 26

Learn More 30

Index 31

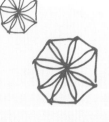

Do You Want to Play a Game?

Do you play games on a computer or phone? Have you played a game on an iPad, a Wii U, or an Xbox? Then you play online games! Online games are games that you play through an **Internet connection** on a computer or a mobile device such as a smartphone or tablet. Some online games help teach reading, spelling, or math skills. Other online games let you dress up cartoon characters or hit home runs into a roaring crowd. There are even games that let you make up characters to play in an online world.

You play some online games by yourself. Other games you can play with a friend across town, across the country, or in another part of the world! These you access through a **video-game console** such as Xbox.

Why Gamers Play

Gamers have many reasons to play online games. Games can be changed often so that they never get boring. You can play them alone or with friends. Since they are played inside, online games can be played no matter how cold, rainy, snowy, or dark it is outside.

Online games can also help players learn valuable skills. To complete quests on Poptropica, gamers use their problem-solving skills. In the game Neopets, players take care of

Many kids enjoy playing online games with their friends. Who can get the highest score?

online pets. This is good practice for taking care of a living pet. Online games also teach players that if you want to win, it is important to practice and to plan.

SAFETY TIP!

Good games can help you build important skills such as planning, making decisions, practicing, and solving problems. Choose your games wisely!

Different Types of Games

You can find online games in many places. Some are on Web sites. Others are played on video-game consoles such as Xbox or PlayStation.

Casual Games

Casual games are simple games you can play just by visiting a Web site. These games usc tools in your **Internet browser** to play sounds and graphics. They are not complicated. You just click and play. You should not need to set up an

SAFETY TIP!

Be careful when you search the Internet for games on Web sites. Only visit sites that you know are safe.

account to play these games. If a game asks you to sign in to play, ask an adult before entering any information about yourself.

Casual games are often found on the Web sites of zoos, museums, TV shows, and magazines. Others are on sites made just for games, such as brainpop.com and funbrain.com. These sites have fun, challenging games that teach reading and math skills.

Networks and Consoles

If you like to race cars, play football, or build Minecraft worlds with your friend across town, you probably use a video-game console.

Funbrain.com has games that help you practice your math and reading skills.

Game systems such as Wii U, PlayStation, and Xbox can be used to play online. These video-game consoles use Internet connections to access a **network** for these games. An adult must sign up for you to become part of a system's network.

Once online, you can **download** games and videos. You can even set up your own **avatar** or character. These games are online, so you can't always be sure who you are playing with. It is safest to play only with friends you know in person.

Massively Multiplayer

Some online games, such as World of Warcraft, have thousands of players who all play together at the same time. These games are called massively multiplayer online games, or MMOs. Many people enjoy this kind of game because they allow players to make avatars, to chat with other

SAFETY TIP!

Have a family video-game night to show
your games to the adults in your family.

players, and to play adventure games in which they gain more and more strength.

Two popular kid-friendly MMOs are Marvel Super Hero Squad and Club Penguin. Marvel Super Hero Squad is a virtual world where players create their own super hero team and go on missions to protect the city from evil villians. Club Penguin players make penguin avatars that play games, make friends, and even have pets! When you play these games, you know you are playing in a safe, bully-free environment.

SAFETY TIP!

Ask a parent to help you set up an account in a kid-friendly MMO. You will be able to chat safely and set up a secure profile.

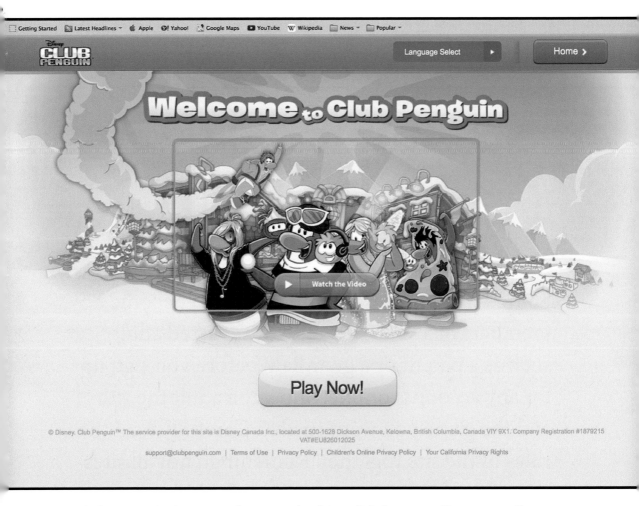

Club Penguin is a popular massively multiplayer online game for kids. You need an adult to create an account for you.

Gaming Safety

° °

Some online games require players to become members of a Web site. Talk to a trusted adult, such as a parent or a guardian, before you sign up for any accounts online. Show the adult the site and the game you want to play. Carefully read the rules of the site together. Remember, not all sites are safe and many are not meant for kids.

If you do sign up, pick a screen name that hides your real name. Never pick a screen name that is close to your real name or one that will give away

Keep your identity safe. Never include personal information in your screen name that could help strangers figure out who you are or where you live.

Never answer personal questions from strangers, even if they seem like fun gaming buddies.

your e-mail address. Choose general information about yourself for a screen name rather than specific, personal information. Use SportsGirl (the fact that you like sports) rather than RedHawk51 (the name of your softball team and your number).

Gaming Bullies

Playing online games is fun. However, when you play with people you do not know, you may run into **griefers**. Griefers are people who make playing games anything but fun. Griefers are gamers who are also bullies. They play to mess up

Griefers think it is fun to make other players feel angry and frustrated. Report them to the Web site's moderator.

a game, break rules, and make trouble for other players.

Other players use online games to try to meet people in real life. These players want to know your age, real name, or password. They may ask to see a picture of you. They may even pretend to be someone you know. These people are predators, and what they do is wrong. Do not share personal information with another player. Do not agree to meet someone in person whom you met online. People online may not be who they seem. Keep online games online!

Getting Help

If someone bullies you, you may feel angry or hurt. But before taking action, tell an adult what has happened. Report the problem to the site's **moderator**.

SAFETY TIP!

Play online games with friends you know in person. That way you will have people with whom you can safely play online.

If a griefer bothers you or an online predator wants to meet you in person, tell an adult immediately!

It is smart to report when other players are behaving badly. That way you can help keep the game safe for yourself and for other players. Most games offer ways players can help keep griefers away. For example, Club Penguin players who have been playing the game for 30 days can become "secret agents" who help keep the game safe.

Do not blame yourself for the way griefers act. And do not feel bad for reporting them. You have done nothing wrong. In fact, by taking action, you can help prevent griefers from picking on other people too!

Set Limits

It is easy to get caught up in an online game. Getting to the next level, earning more tokens, or beating the top score may seem like the most important thing in the world. But it's not. If you find yourself playing games or thinking about playing games all the time, take a break. Go for a bike ride, play with your friends, get something to eat, or finish up your homework. Don't put off the other important things in your life to spend all your time playing games.

Online games are fun, but make sure you do not spend all your time playing them!

Online gaming should not be your only activity. Invite your family to spend a day at the beach!

Decide ahead of time how long you will play your game. Set a timer or an alarm, then stop when it goes off. Don't spend more than two hours each day in front of a computer or TV screen. Instead, play basketball, walk your dog, or go to the park. If you cannot go outside, play a board game, draw, paint, read, or listen to music. Online games are lots of fun. So is spending time with your friends and family.

SAFETY TIP!

Think of fun activities you can do with your family and friends that don't require a screen.

Learn More

Books

Harbour, Jonathan S. *Video Game Programming for Kids.* New York: Cengage Learning, 2012.

Schrier, Allyson Valentine. *Gaming Safely.* Mankato, Minn: Capstone Press, 2013.

Web Sites

pbskids.org/cyberchase/math-games/

Free, safe online math games and puzzles.

primarygames.com

Free learning games for kids.

fbi.gov/fun-games/kids/kids-safety

Online safety tips for kids from the Federal Bureau of Investigation.

Index

A
accounts, 12, 18

B
brainpop.com, 12
bullies, 20, 22

C
casual games, 11, 12
Club Penguin, 16, 25

F
family, 15, 29
friends, 8, 14, 16, 26, 29
funbrain.com, 12

G
griefers, 20, 25

I
iPad, 7

M
Marvel Super Hero Squad, 16
Minecraft, 12
MMOs, 14, 16
moderators, 22

N
Neopets, 8
networks, 14

P
passwords, 22
PlayStation, 11, 14
Poptropica, 8
problem-solving skills, 8, 10

R
rules, 18, 22

S
screen names, 18, 20
secret agents, 25
smartphones, 7

W
Web sites, 11, 12, 18
Wii U, 7, 14
World of Warcraft, 14

X
Xbox, 7, 8, 11, 14

Published in 2016 by Enslow Publishing, LLC.
101 W. 23rd Street, Suite 240, New York, NY 10011

Library of Congress Cataloging-in-Publication Data
Yearling, Tricia.
 How do I play games online? / Tricia Yearling.
    pages cm. — (Online smarts)
 Includes bibliographical references and index.
 Summary: "Discusses how kids can safely play games online"—Provided by publisher.
 ISBN 978-0-7660-6847-6 (library binding)
 ISBN 978-0-7660-6845-2 (pbk.)
 ISBN 978-0-7660-6846-9 (6-pack)
 1. Internet games—Safety measures—Juvenile literature. 2. Internet and children—Safety
measures—Juvenile literature. 3. Internet—Security measures—Juvenile literature. I. Title.
 GV1469.15.Y43 2015
 004.67'8083—dc23
                          2015007453

Printed in the United States of America

To Our Readers: We have done our best to make sure all Web sites in this book were active and
appropriate when we went to press. However, the author and the publisher have no control over
and assume no liability for the material available on those Web sites or on any Web sites they may
link to. Any comments or suggestions can be sent by e-mail to customerservice@enslow.com.

Photo Credits: Creatista/Shutterstock.com, p. 15; Elena Kalistratova/iStock/Thinkstock (chapter
opener and front and back matter); Giulio Fornasar/Shutterstock.com, p. 27; Günay Mutlu/
E+/Getty Images, p. 19; Jovan Mandic/Shutterstock.com, p. 6; Kei Uesugi/Photodisk/Getty
Images, p. 28; Peter Dazeley/The Image Bank/Getty Images, p. 21; Purestock/Getty Images, p. 24;
Purestock/Thinkstock (series logo), p. 3; Rob Marmion/Shutterstock, p. 18; Robert Dant/E+/
Getty Images, p. 5; Sashatigar/iStock/Thinkstock (doodle art on contents page and fact boxes);
Sean Locke Photogaphy/Shutterstock.com (boy), p. 3; Sergey Novikov/Shutterstock.com, p. 9;
Shouoshu/iStock/Thinkstock (digital background), p. 3; Stefano Tinti/Shutterstock.com; 23.

Cover Credits: Purestock/Thinkstock (series logo); Sean Locke Photogaphy/Shutterstock.com
(boy); Shouoshu/iStock/Thinkstock (digital background).